# TALES OF TERROR'S
# FRANKENSTEIN REVIEWED
## 2020 EDITION

STEVE HUTCHISON

# FRANKENSTEIN

## REVIEWED

### 2020 EDITION

**FEATURING**

**STEVE HUTCHISON**

CRITIC

First Printing: 2020
ISBN-13: 978-1654773816


Bookstores and wholesalers: Please contact books@terror.ca.

Tales of Terror
tales@terror.ca
www.terror.ca

# INTRODUCTION

Horror critic Steve Hutchison analyzes 39 Frankenstein movies. How many have you seen? Each article includes a synopsis, five different ratings, and a review.

# CONTENT

# #1
# FRANKENSTEIN

## 1931

A scientist gives life to a creature made of parts from exhumed corpses.

| | | |
|---:|:---:|:---|
| STARS |  | **4/8** |
| STORY | | **5/8** |
| CREATIVITY | | **8/8** |
| ACTING | | **6/8** |
| QUALITY | | **5/8** |

Frankenstein is a high-end adaptation of a novel by the same title written by novelist Mary Shelley. Many hands handled this script in order to create a horror masterpiece that calls upon our darkest fears. By protagonizing its monster, it informs us on the grey zones of its evil. The character is written as instinctive but unintelligent. He is a supernatural brute brought back from the afterlife.

The monster's design is memorable and highly marketable. Sumptuous matte painting is used to support his evolving state of mind. The set design suggests a surreal aura that augments his presence. He isn't unlike Dracula, but was born from technology and is a glorified bully; not a hypnotist. The cast is limited but effective and focused. The leads, particularly, deliver an intense performance.

The castle most of the action takes place in is dark and claustrophobic. Production design did a great job of building a futuristic laboratory that sets the table for thrilling action scenes and two acts filled with special effects appearing ahead of their time. The writing and directing are impeccable and barely struggle with the technical challenges such a ground-breaking concept poses.

**#2**

# THE BRIDE OF FRANKENSTEIN

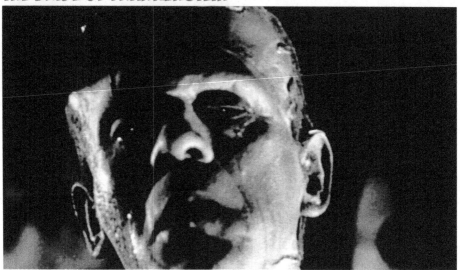

## 1935

Two scientists experimenting with the afterlife bait one of their creations with another.

STARS  **3/8**
STORY **3/8**
CREATIVITY **8/8**
ACTING **6/8**
QUALITY **5/8**

Contrary to what we presumed once 1931's Frankenstein's end credits rolled, the protagonist isn't dead and his creature is on the loose. We get confirmation on this during the first scenes. We soon revisit sumptuous surreal sets of castles and forests. This film relies on sound stages so much to furnish its backdrop that it comes out as charmingly fake.

Most of the cast got renewed but the monster is still played by legend Boris Karloff. An idea is thrown that the monster can be calmed or neutralized by feminine presence. The "bride" from the title in fact gets little screen time, but makes every second count. Her design is as marketable as the first monster's, though it doesn't inspire fear. This sequel would rather have you cry than shiver.

The original monster has been tamed and doesn't come out as psychopathic anymore. He is more a sensible brute than a demon, here, and is given more depth. The film isn't as iconic or memorable as the original classic, but the photography, the ambiance and the pacing are similar. It is sometimes at the brink of parody, sometimes too slow, but it redeems itself with a firework in the third act.

# #3

# SON OF FRANKENSTEIN

## 1939

The son of a mad scientist revives the monster his father created before his death.

| | | |
|---:|:--:|:--|
| STARS | ⬠ | **3/8** |
| STORY | 📖 | **3/8** |
| CREATIVITY | 💡 | **8/8** |
| ACTING | 🎭 | **6/8** |
| QUALITY | 🏅 | **5/8** |

The monster was plentifully exposed in Bride of Frankenstein and is no longer a creepy mystery to us. We fast forward in the future, here, and people refer to him as a vague folktale; an urban legend. His body is soon found, though, and it triggers a sequence of events not unlike the original Universal original adaptation. The tone is the same, the structure is similar and the acting is up to par.

The film is sprinkled with fun surprises and twists that add a lot to the story. Returning characters make us care about what ends up being half a sequel, half a re-imagining. The dialogue is more serious, this time around, and wants us to savor apprehending the angry monster's resuscitation. The movie prefers long discussions over tense moments and has a frustrating amount of padding material.

Good performances get us through the filler so we can enjoy a satisfying third act. The photography and the effects are crisper than ever, yet the sets are dark and not revealing as much splendor as the two previous Universal Frankenstein movies did. The running time is significantly longer, allowing for more character development and a slow burning pace.

**#4**

# THE GHOST OF FRANKENSTEIN

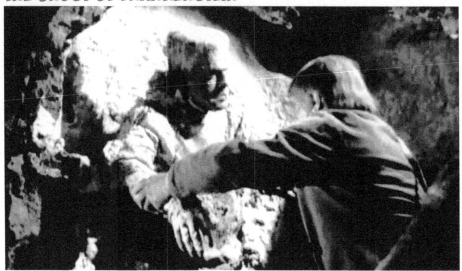

## 1942

A son of scientists attempts brain transplant on a revenant.

STARS ⭐ **3/8**

STORY 📖 **5/8**

CREATIVITY 💡 **8/8**

ACTING 🎭 **6/8**

QUALITY 🏅 **5/8**

As we learned in the previous movie, Ygor's most evil rendition can control the monster with his flute, injecting a magical element into a horror tale that used to treat science rather than the occult as fantasy. This is also the most political approach to Frankenstein by Universal Studios. It goes as far as debating whether the franchise's antagonist should die or be left alone.

The odd chemistry between Ygor and his creature benefits from the unexpected role reversal. It's a fun twist on a story many times retold and susceptible to redundancy, and it makes the monster appear more threatening than he did in previous installments. The makers don't feel a necessity to make him sympathetic and rekindle his scaring potential, instead.

We still get claustrophobic castle sets, a cyberpunk scientific lab, a crazy doctor, but this Frankenstein adaptation takes all the right liberties to spice up an already acquired taste. It takes many chances and mostly succeeds where it gambles. It gives us an updated yet simplified horror icon that matches Dracula's evil and doesn't feel the need to protagonize evil in order to win us over.

## #5

# FRANKENSTEIN MEETS THE WOLF MAN

## 1943

A werewolf travels to find a man who can lift his curse.

STARS  3/8

STORY 4/8

CREATIVITY 8/8

ACTING 6/8

QUALITY 5/8

This movie focuses more on the wolf than the revenant. An idea is thrown suggesting that the werewolf's curse can be lifted by using Frankenstein's technology. Meanwhile, citizens are throwing blames at Frankenstein for the murders his creature committed. This culminates in both creatures, wolf and revenant, meeting each other. The decent script takes care of making this improbability seamless.

What a title! Surprisingly, the movie's not any dumber than the previous installments of both franchises. The two worlds, as it turns out, are perfectly interchangeable. They blend well together in style and quality. We get fun, minimalistic transformation scenes, a surreal castle and fantastic sets of fake forests. Both characters can therefore reside and shine in their respective element.

Lon Chaney Jr. played both the last creature and the last Wolf Man on screen. He can only pick one character and decides to return as the latter. This film is a mess when it comes to continuity, but the story keeps us entertained regardless. Will the two monsters fight each other or cooperate to overcome a common enemy? There's only one way to know! Watch out for that third act. It's a delight!

# #6

# HOUSE OF FRANKENSTEIN

## 1944

A scientist and a hunchback escape from prison and encounter a vampire, a werewolf and a revenant.

STARS 4/8

STORY 4/8

CREATIVITY 8/8

ACTING 6/8

QUALITY 5/8

Most actors in House of Frankenstein give a fluid performance. The main protagonists are renditions of Dr. Frankenstein and Ygor. Their fate intertwines with Mary Shelley's revenant, Bram Stoker's vampire and Curt Siodmak's werewolf. The match-up's title can be misleading because the three antagonists are equally important and because this is a sequel to all three Universal Studios franchises.

The casting is appropriate. You get Boris Karloff, Lon Chaney Jr. and John Carradine on top of their game. They've played these interchangeable roles before, but not in a comedy. The human to bat metamorphoses are borrowed from Son of Dracula, so they're decent but not convincing. The special effects generally show improvement, but the transitions aren't great.

So, three horror icons were turned into an inside joke. The story is fun to sit through but can't be taken seriously. It ties in with 1943's Frankenstein Meets the Wolf Man and introduces the two other Universal monsters to humor. It's a film made for the fan that makes fun of its own legacy and offers variations on its own tropes in slapstick fashion.

## #7

# HOUSE OF DRACULA

## 1945

A werewolf and a vampire seek help from a scientist they believe can cure their respective affliction.

STARS ⭐ **4/8**

STORY 📖 **3/8**

CREATIVITY 💡 **8/8**

ACTING 🎭 **6/8**

QUALITY 🏅 **5/8**

Lon Chaney returns as the wolf man and shape shifts inside a jail cell; fully exposed and witnessed by many. Meanwhile, Count Dracula does shady business. Frankenstein, on the other hand, is the same tender brute but slightly dumber. The new hunchback, present in most Frankenstein adaptations, is played by a woman and is one of the creepiest variations of her interchangeable archetype.

The movie is eerie but not scary. In a nutshell, it is a condensed and polished version of every cliche originating from all three Universal Studio franchises, and more so, even, than 1944's House of Frankenstein. Continuity is an issue but should be ignored at this point. The previous sequels were repetitive and all monsters have been many times recast with great exchangeable actors.

The set design is big and luxurious; something we lost for a while, along with some of the ambiance. The lighting is just right. Photography and effects show global improvement, too. The story is silly but the title and promo alone allude to fun times, good energy and genuine acting, writing and directing from horror monuments. We get it all! Expect an action perspective and not straight horror.

## #8

# BUD ABBOTT LOU COSTELLO MEET FRANKENSTEIN

## 1948

Two freight handlers encounter a vampire and a revenant.

STARS 4/8

STORY 2/8

CREATIVITY 7/8

ACTING 6/8

QUALITY 5/8

Here, Abbott and Costello turn legendary Universal monsters into a parody of themselves. They aren't their evil and powerful self, anymore, and they're no longer scary. Having two slapstick kings fight infamous horror figures who share the antagonist part is a sexy idea and the makers make the most of it. They do not bother with continuity, focusing on mood and characters instead.

Abbot and Costello have been through over twenty screen adventures at this point and are still going strong. They are a sympathetic duo who, by their innocence and natural sense of humor, offer a passive but serious resistance to fear and horror. They make this feel-good comedy somewhat a testament to the preatomic monsters who were replaced by giants, mutants and disasters.

Great talent and imagination went into this production. This clash of genre, much like a play, is meticulously blocked, written and directed in way to inspire fun, excitement and to let the audience in on the joke. The film is a fast-paced sequence of nearly inconsequential isolated scenes that stretch to no end so that Costello can fix trouble by causing twice as much.

**#9**

# THE CURSE OF FRANKENSTEIN

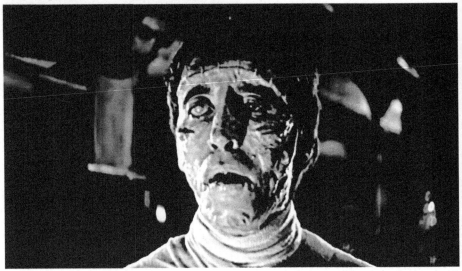

## 1957

A creature brought to life by a scientist becomes brutal and out of control.

STARS ⭐ **4/8**

STORY 📖 **5/8**

CREATIVITY 💡 **7/8**

ACTING 🎭 **6/8**

QUALITY 🏅 **6/8**

As opposed to Dracula, a product of the occult, Frankenstein is a story about bringing back the dead through science. Hammer Films bring their own vision of the creature, in tones of auburn, grey and blood. It is indeed gorier than most adaptations of the classic novel and just as shocking. In this Gothic film, Peter Cushing does the talking and Christopher Lee handles the physical performances.

The sets are sumptuous, evenly lit; creating a unique ambiance. Sexier than Universal's rendition, Curse of Frankenstein gives importance to the different character bonds. This is, after all, a love tragedy as much as it is a monster movie and the slow pace establishes that early on. The performers are entertaining and, so, the procedural structure isn't an issue.

This is a period piece with a particular aesthetic, a unique score, and consequential ambiance. Heavily textured and photographically dense, the image is as rich as the script and the dialogue bits. You'll enjoy the vibe, admire the performances and get immersed in the set design, but the slow pace will be a deal-breaker unless you're going into this knowing it keeps the best for last.

## #10

# THE REVENGE OF FRANKENSTEIN

## 1958

Released from his death sentence, a scientist returns to the illegal experiments he was convicted for.

STARS 4/8

STORY 4/8

CREATIVITY 6/8

ACTING 6/8

QUALITY 6/8

It's with apprehension of things to come that we enter Dr. Frankenstein's world for the second time in this now official sub-franchise. The last movie covered the classic story, so this one is free to explore new territories in storytelling, gore and taboos. It is more intellectual and more a scientific procedural than its predecessor. Ambiance, performances and photography are matched.

We get to the gruesome much faster, this time around, with Frankenstein having learned nothing from his past experiences and shortly getting back to them. The dialogue is still well written and delivered. The same level of quality can be found in the set design work. The characters and their arc are unusual and, while the film is slow and chatty, we end up caring about their dark fate.

Christopher Lee, the monster from Curse of Frankenstein, is nowhere in sight. He was replaced by a poorly designed and cast protagonized revenant that inspires neither fear nor disgust. While the film isn't exactly boring, in the end, not a lot happens. The story is straight-forward and any attempt at romance or exposition fills like obligatory filler.

# #11

# THE EVIL OF FRANKENSTEIN

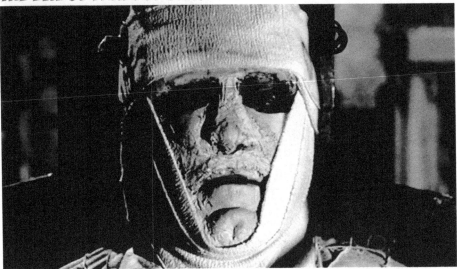

## 1964

A scientist attempts to bring back the dead with the help of his assistant and a hypnotist.

STARS  4/8

STORY 4/8

CREATIVITY 7/8

ACTING 6/8

QUALITY 6/8

Peter Cushing reprises the role of Frankenstein in this second sequel to Hammer Films' adaptation of the Mary Shelley novel. It is taking an increasing amount of liberties in regards to gore and controversy, spicing up a typically conservative plot. This is yet another beautiful period piece with vibrant matte painting and gorgeous Gothic set design.

You can find grander effects in this than the previous entries, mostly when it comes to Frankenstein's laboratory. There is a good deal of eye candy sprinkled from beginning to end, which helps keep up entertained. The tighter pace doesn't hurt. The new monster looks great when filmed under the right light. Its allure is somewhat reminiscent of the Universal Studios monster and he's kind of scary.

We never go into a Frankenstein adaptation or sequel expecting twists and turns. We can already predict the outcome, so we're all about the directing and singular aesthetic. The Evil of Frankenstein achieves this. It lives up to its tradition and the public's expectations. While it'll generally feel like more of the same, many significant technical improvements show.

# #12

# FRANKENSTEIN VS. BARAGON

## 1965

During WWII, two giants fight each other.

STARS 2/8
STORY 2/8
CREATIVITY 7/8
ACTING 4/8
QUALITY 3/8

So somehow, at some point, Frankenstein's monster gets turned into a kaiju. How we get to that point needs to be seen and it isn't exactly simple. The pretext is shoved down our throats with a few lines of dialogue and some aspirin. It's harder to absorb than the horrendous props and miniature sets that get destroyed throughout this film. Ironically, destruction is what we came here for.

For what seems like eternity, we try to figure out who the protagonists are. The scientists look like good guys but they're responsible for this mayhem. The army means well but is at war with Frankenstein's creature. Frankenstein creature is more dumb than innocent. Then, there is Baragon, the second kaiju. Godzilla had more worthy foes. Baragon looks like an amateur!

Despite its many flaws, this film is entertaining. It has a bunch of extras who can hardly dance, who can't act scared and who move as a single entity. The editing is innocent. It overuses dissolves and fades to black. Like most kaiju films, this one contains very little actual kaiju action. We spend most of our time with different groups of people doing God knows what until the final showdown.

# #13
# JESSE JAMES MEETS FRANKENSTEIN'S DAUGHTER

## 1966

An Old West outlaw finds refuge in a castle where resuscitation experiments are conducted.

STARS ⭐ **3/8**

STORY 📖 **3/8**

CREATIVITY 💡 **6/8**

ACTING 🎭 **5/8**

QUALITY 🏅 **4/8**

All significant characters are introduced fifteen minutes in. Jesse James contrasts with Billy the Kid, from Billy the Kid Versus Dracula, in that he is classy; not bratty. The two Western horror films are equal parts of a homogeneous double feature. Jesse James Meets Frankenstein's Daughter is the better one. It is structured more naturally and it is more dynamic.

The tongue-in-cheek humor hinted at in the title doesn't exactly match the ambiance. This isn't really a comedy. Like Billy the Kid Versus Dracula, 1966's Jesse James Meets Frankenstein's Daughter is an awkward but ambitious concoction of famous Hollywood genre tropes. It is heavily flawed and looks cheap, yet it can intermittently afford high-end sets, costumes and matte painting.

You have to leave your brain at the door for this one, and appreciate the rare mix of steampunk and Western cinema. Marie Frankenstein is an interesting rendition of the mad scientist stereotype, but Igor isn't his crippled self. The monster's design is simple but gets the job done. The evil trinity appears dissociated from the main plot until the 3rd act, when all hell finally breaks loose.

## #14

# FRANKENSTEIN CREATED WOMAN

## 1967

Once re-animated by his assistant, a scientist becomes inspired by the idea of soul containment.

STARS 4/8

STORY 4/8

CREATIVITY 6/8

ACTING 6/8

QUALITY 6/8

Frankenstein Created Woman goes beyond the concept of the evil re-animated corpse and presents an intrigue that revolves around containment of the soul, instead. The subject at hand is interesting but underdeveloped considering where the writers could go with the premise. It is downplaying the visuals and the scares, but, as a supernatural thriller, it pulls no punches.

It takes its unique spot in the franchise by displaying female partial nudity, throwing in a lengthy awkward bar fight not typical to the subgenre, and pushing controversy and gore generally further than previously attempted. It conforms to the previous films in terms of photo, set design, and, most importantly, brings back the excellent Peter Cushing as Baron Frankenstein.

So, they made the creature a woman this time! 1935's Bride of Frankenstein had the same gimmick. Sadly, by making her beautiful and not horrific, the creators ended up with somewhat of a femme fatale, not a brutal aberration. Her screen time as a monster is negligible, too, which is confusing. Things get tense in the last act only, so better gear up for all that dialogue!

## #15

# FRANKENSTEIN MUST BE DESTROYED

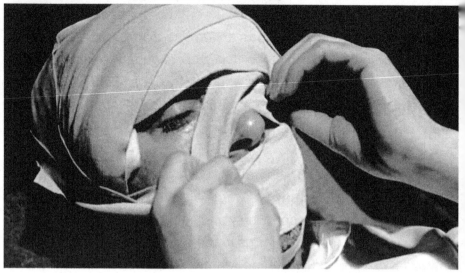

## 1969

A scientist plots to perform brain transplant on a mental patient.

STARS ⛥ **4/8**

STORY 📖 **3/8**

CREATIVITY 💡 **5/8**

ACTING 😀 **6/8**

QUALITY 🏅 **6/8**

Rather on the slow and chatty side, this fifth installment in Hammer's interpretations of Frankenstein tells a story of resuscitation through brain transplant. Like all the sequels that came before, it attempts to stand out while giving you more of what you like under the same lighting and desaturation: a sometimes bloody, sometimes tense and always posh period piece filmed just right.

Frankenstein turns into a rapist, now, of all things, boosting his criminal record and reminding us that he is the bad guy and always was, no matter how sympathetic Peter Cushing's act would have us believe otherwise. The cinematography is still very oppressive, atmospheric, bearing the sumptuous Hammer signature and offering a rationalized revision of Mary Shelley's legacy.

You'll have to wait until the second half for things to really pick up, and then another while for monster action to kick in, at which point you'll realize you went through a lot of dialogue for nothing. While the writers managed to pull another variant on the classic tale, it feels we're in a dead end. It's too little too late. This is indeed one of the weakest sequels in the franchise.

# #16
# THE HORROR OF FRANKENSTEIN

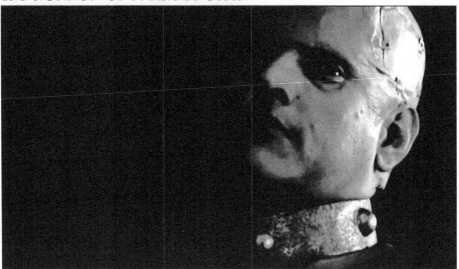

## 1970

A scientist illegally acquires dead human limbs in order to assemble a revenant.

STARS 3/8
STORY 3/8
CREATIVITY 5/8
ACTING 6/8
QUALITY 5/8

The Horror of Frankenstein is first in its collection not to feature Peter Cushing as the main protagonist. As such, it somewhat feels like a pale remake of Curse of Frankenstein. His abrupt absence brings up too much confusion. We've come to take the man for granted; the franchise's continuity was always hermetic. This is better seen as a stand-alone film, independent from the previous streak.

The unusual dialogue and relationships between the different players sometimes translates into unconfessed, lightly comedic homoerotic scenes, questionable partnerships and awkward love relationships, making The Horror of Frankenstein surreal, almost parodic of its predecessors, but without ever labeling itself as a comedy. This kind of sexual tension wasn't previously attempted; only eluded to.

It's a nice retelling that comes with potential deceptions. It constitutes a breach of continuity in the storyline, for those who care, and succeeds better as reboot than it does as a sequel. It has been a while since we've seen a good looking monster, though, and you'll have to wait before you get to it. This is a slow film with a lot of filler and is the biggest nail in the coffin, so far.

# #17

# DRACULA VS. FRANKENSTEIN

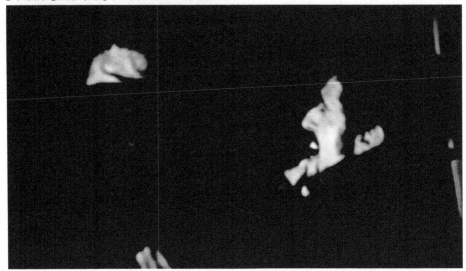

## 1971

A vampire asks a mad scientist to re-animate a corpse.

STARS 2/8
STORY 2/8
CREATIVITY 7/8
ACTING 3/8
QUALITY 3/8

The title is more interesting than the film itself. Dracula vs. Frankenstein has confusing cinematography, unflattering photography, is poorly lit, badly framed, features uncomfortable dialogue, unnatural blocking and has a weird staging. The special effects are laughable, behind their time, and the characters range from boring to awkward. This is a strange exploitation flick filled with missteps.

Those are some of the weakest renditions of Dracula and Frankenstein's monster in cinema history, yet some of the funniest. The script is disorganized, takes too many directions and gets lost in the details. The more tolerable parts happen in Frankenstein's fun house, a place filled with monsters, cadavers and various death simulations. In vain, though, this barely ties in with the main plot.

Lon Chaney Jr. plays Groton, a poor man's version of Igor; an ax murderer, precisely. Though his motivations aren't clear, he somewhat turns an otherwise dry horror movie into a gory slasher. If you're hoping for a duel between Dracula and Frankenstein's revenant, look elsewhere. There are more bullies, brutes, bikers, rapists and hippies, here, than actual supernatural face-offs.

# #18

# LADY FRANKENSTEIN

## 1971

A surgeon resumes her father's brain transplant experiments after his death.

STARS 3/8

STORY 4/8

CREATIVITY 6/8

ACTING 5/8

QUALITY 5/8

This movie isn't terribly scary, but it sure gets unintentionally funny. The monster's costume is often fully lit, revealing how poorly it was designed. The use of foul language doesn't coincide with the era, this being a Gothic period piece, and scenes right out of a soft core porno are guaranteed to distract the audience in the midst of serious dialogue.

There is a lot of scientific hocus-pocus in various conversations, in the set design and in the props used, yet the movie takes itself surprisingly seriously. The romance feels forced, useless and exists only to turn Nadia into a ruthless seductress. Her charm makes her a more successful murderer and gives her the opportunity to show some skin. The script needs nudity to move forward...

The title, "Lady Frankenstein", doesn't imply that the monster is a female but, rather, that the mad doctor is replaced by his daughter, a surgeon, after his death. This is certainly not the best Frankenstein movie out there, but it is not the worst either. It is entertaining, even if only for its constant goofiness. It is fun, sexy and not very gory. It has its own signature and a memorable one.

# #19
# BLACKENSTEIN

## 1973

A medical surgery turns a war amputee into a monster.

STARS ✪ **2/8**

STORY 📖 **2/8**

CREATIVITY 💡 **6/8**

ACTING 😃 **3/8**

QUALITY 🏅 **3/8**

There is no blaxploitation vibe, per say, to Blakenstein. The monster's ethnicity is irrelevant to the plot, contrary to 1972's Blacula. This is a straight horror drama with no tongue-in-cheek elements, so the title is barely deserved. It has a washed out photography, barely decorated set design, poor storytelling and embarrassing dialogue. The audio is terrible and the camera work even worse.

The acting is awkward and probably answers to poor directing. There is no film language, here. The camera is hysterical, offers bad angles, bad framing, amateur blocking and centers on the subject compulsively. The film is not tense, not scary, but at least follows the Frankenstein story. Sadly, the monster doesn't look like a monster; no effort went into a decent make-up.

The makers can't establish an ambiance, so they often resort to loud music that is too intense for what actually happens on screen. It is so loud that it buries the dialogue, which is probably a good thing anyway. The actors seem embarrassed. The film doesn't know what it wants to be and what tone it should have so it chooses chaos. This little exploitation film is one step away from a disaster.

# #20

# FRANKENSTEIN: THE TRUE STORY

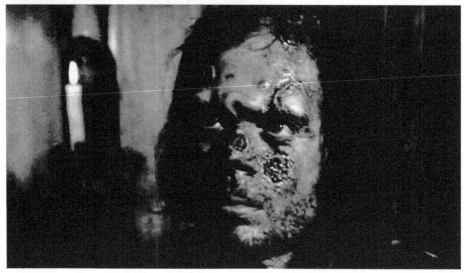

## 1973

A scientist gives life to a creature he realizes he cannot control.

STARS 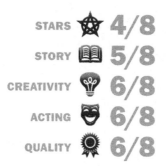 4/8

STORY 5/8

CREATIVITY 6/8

ACTING 6/8

QUALITY 6/8

A narrator introduces us to this lengthy story by presenting it as an intellectual adaptation of the popular Mary Shelly novel. He reminds us that the author was only nineteen years old when she wrote the book. During his speech, we see a montage of what we presume are the best parts of the film and we're not far off. This is the ultimate slow burn and it just got spoiled!

The filmmakers have some big shoes to fill. First, this is a TV movie. Second, it is three hours long. Third, it claims to appeal to our intellect more than the average Frankenstein adaptation. The inevitable happens; this ends up being a stretched out version of your typical Frankenstein movie. The filmmakers more or less meet their objectives. This flick is, I'm afraid, forgettable.

Since the pacing is slow, every phase of this film comes with preliminaries. Frankenstein: The True Story is presented in two parts. Both are dialogue heavy, big on costumes and old architecture, and both are melodramatic. The actors pull it off extremely well. The photography is surprisingly good for a TV movie. The dialogue is smart. The script is competent. The directing is irreproachable.

**#21**

# FLESH FOR FRANKENSTEIN

## 1973

A scientist and his assistant attempt to create a superior race of walking corpses.

STARS ✪ **5/8**

STORY 📖 **2/8**

CREATIVITY 💡 **7/8**

ACTING 😄 **6/8**

QUALITY 🏅 **5/8**

Flesh for Frankenstein is a darkly eroticised version of a classic tale that was many times adapted but never as eccentrically depicted. The homoerotic, or rather bi-erotic subtext writes itself when it comes to Frankenstein, but most have stayed away from it or vaguely alluded to it. Mary Shelley's premise comes with sexual ambiguity and grey zones that this film explores with a grin.

More shocking than the on-screen content is how great the movie looks and how well executed it is considering all its taboos. The writing, the directing and the acting are unusual, awkward, but always even and fully mastered. The underlying BDSM reminiscence is the ultimate deal-breaker for any audience, here. Flesh for Frankenstein is both titillating and disgusting. Even the gore looks sexy...

This unlikely period piece has one of the best decorated sets found in Frankenstein films. It is flattered by keen photography and an atmosphere you could cut with a knife. It is uncomfortably lit on purpose and never hides its visual flaws in black shadows. What you get from this film will depend on your sexual perspective, preferences, your love for oddities and your flexibility as a horror fan.

#22

# FRANKENSTEIN AND THE MONSTER FROM HELL

## 1973

An incarcerated scientist who discovered the formula to resuscitation recruits an apprentice to carry his legacy.

STARS ✪ **4/8**

STORY 📖 **5/8**

CREATIVITY 💡 **6/8**

ACTING 😃 **6/8**

QUALITY ☀ **6/8**

Before Peter Cushing was replaced by a vague parodic copy of himself, in the previous installment, he, just like his creations, became one of the undead and somewhat antagonized as the franchise's arc progressed. Well, he's back and he's crazier; more inquisitive, dominant, eerier than ever. The great asylum sets reinforce his presence. Their visual oppression is stunning.

The same could be said about the monster design if more effort would've gone into make-up. The rubber mask isn't always seamless. Sadly, you can see the actor behind the cheap mask under most lighting. We've seen better. The Gothic sets and matte painting are a marvel. The gore is okay. The film gets increasingly dark and interesting once you're passed the first half, so it requires patience.

Frankenstein and the Monster from Hell surpasses some of the previous sequels. The story is denser and highly creative, considering the rigid Hammer brand continuity. The performances are a treat. The parts are well scripted and the dialogue holds up. The series feels a little tired, now; we're obviously rehashing the same recipe, trying new spices, but it's the sauce that keeps us coming back.

# #23

# SON OF DRACULA

## 1974

A vampire falls in love with a human and finds himself in conflict with a revenant.

STARS  3/8

STORY 2/8

CREATIVITY 6/8

ACTING 4/8

QUALITY 4/8

Son of Dracula is modern in that it takes nothing seriously despite featuring classic monsters like vampires, Igor and Frankenstein's creature. The title cards are the second reason we understand this is a contemporary tale, as we're transported through time, as if taken by the hand. The last clue is a crowd intermittently dancing at the disco to the sound of a band. Yes, this is a musical.

Why all the music, you ask? Harry Nilsson and Ringo Starr star in Son of Dracula. Starr plays an embarassing version of Merlin the Magician and Nilsson plays Count Downe. Get it? Laughing, yet? The deeper you venture into this story, the more confused you get, mostly because this is a portfolio for two musicians, which causes music to take priority over common sense.

The werewolf costume isn't too bad. Most creatures look decent but are underexposed. The effects team just didn't try that hard. The film is strangely edited, clumsily orchestrated and poorly paced. If you're looking for something unique, you found it. If ambiance matters to you, you found some. If, on the other hand, you're looking for a good story or strong performances, look elsewhere.

# #24

# YOUNG FRANKENSTEIN

## 1974

The descendant of a mad scientist finds the secret to reanimating the dead.

STARS 6/8

STORY 5/8

CREATIVITY 7/8

ACTING 7/8

QUALITY 6/8

Spoof of the early Frankenstein films, and presented in black in white to make it a point, this hilarious slapstick comedy simply couldn't have existed in the conservative years of horror films. As a period piece, it works marvelously. The old cinematographic atmosphere is recreated brilliantly. Research and attention to detail make Young Frankenstein something worth watching.

The castle sets are beautiful and reminiscent of the 30's Universal monster movie look and feel. Gene Wilder's interpretation of Frankenstein is strongly inspired by Colin Clive's from 1931's Frankenstein. His performance dominates the whole production. He is supported by the new Igor, a hilarious hunchback. The monster design is nothing out of the box, but the story is.

Innocent, goofy, vicious, and modernized; the humor in Young Frankenstein is varied and mostly works. It is, in a way, a therapy towards Gothic Hollywood movies that attempts to depict characters more developed than those of the good old classics. It is ironic to compare this comedy to the films it makes fun of, because it achieves many aspects better and without resorting to the fear element.

*#25*

# THE ROCKY HORROR PICTURE SHOW

## 1975

Newlyweds are lured at the center of a mansion where a mad scientist conducts shocking experiments.

| | | |
|---:|:---:|:---|
| STARS | ✪ | **6/8** |
| STORY | 📖 | **4/8** |
| CREATIVITY | 💡 | **7/8** |
| ACTING | 😃 | **7/8** |
| QUALITY | ✹ | **7/8** |

It starts out the way many horror movies do; with a flat tire on a rainy night and a creepy mansion nearby, then slowly turns into a homophobe's worst nightmare, drag queen included. Tim Curry plays an eccentric transvestite and a memorable caricature of Dr. Frankenstein. A variety of great wardrobes, sets and songs make The Rocky Horror Picture Show one of the best horror musicals in history.

It is based on a play by Richard O'Brien who impersonates Riff Raff, an hilarious rendition of Igor. He is to blame for the confusing lyrics and the unusual screenplay, but those oddities make Rocky Horror all the more rewatchable once the twists hit. The end product has a cult quality to it. It is a surreal experience that looks and feels like nothing else.

It has a libertarian vibe that will hit close to home for libertarians, fetishists, fans of BDSM, homosexuals and bisexuals, but will please an audience simply looking for shock value as well. What is sexy to some might trigger jealous memories or repressed thoughts in others. Don't expect a strong script or any kind of tact. Appreciate, instead, an immersing theatrical polished for the screen.

## #26

# THE BRIDE

## 1985

Two undead creatures are introduced to humanity.

STARS  5/8

STORY 5/8

CREATIVITY 6/8

ACTING 7/8

QUALITY 7/8

Two fragile monsters are depicted in 1985's The Bride. They are the good guys discovering what a cruel world they now inhabit. They each follow their own adventure; facing challenges, obstacles and foes. The brilliant screenplay makes their individual journey fun, heart-warming and sad. Rarely have we seen Frankenstein's creatures go through such an emotional roller coaster.

This is a romanticized and heavily polished re-imagining of 1935's The Bride of Frankenstein. It expands beyond the original ending and offers a more positive outlook. Bride "Eva" learns eminence and dignity while monster "Victor" lives as a vagrant. Both story lines converge beautifully, at different times, an aspect writer Lloyd Fonvielle juggles with magnificently.

The Bride isn't exactly a horror movie: it's more of a love story and an adventure film. The plot is ludicrous at times but touching otherwise. The photography is just right, the editing flawless, the set design convincing and the wardrobes spot on. Though it steers away from the typical Frankenstein structure, this adaptation of the classic novel highly impresses on a technical level.

# #27
# FRANKENHOOKER

## 1990

A medical students attempts to re-animate his dead girlfriend using body parts from dismembered prostitutes.

STARS **6/8**

STORY **6/8**

CREATIVITY **8/8**

ACTING **6/8**

QUALITY **6/8**

This parodic take on Frankenstein is everything but old fashioned. It is nicely packaged fun, shock and macabre sprinkled with generous gratuitous nudity. Protagonist Jeffrey Franken turns himself into a mad scientist by strategically drilling holes into his brain, then attempts to mix and match body parts from different prostitutes in order to re-assemble and bring back his dead fiancée.

The film is a delightful succession of hooker jokes. It thoroughly makes fun of drug addictions, pimp clichés and the female body. It treats its gore with hilarious slapstick comedy and exaggerated practical effects. You get death by robotized lawnmower, by explosive narcotics, a dinner for two with a dismembered girlfriend and a bunch more over the top tongue-in-cheek scenes you won't forget.

There is an element of slasher to Frankenhooker. It manifests itself in the last third of the movie. Elizabeth doesn't just smack and choke her "clients"; she electrocutes them and blows them up. Her appearance, tics and M.O. make her one of the most interesting female monsters of modern horror movies. Expect an entertaining story, good reveals, twisted visuals and a memorable ending.

*#28*

# FRANKENSTEIN UNBOUND

## 1990

A scientist travels back in time where he meets a famous monster and the writer who documented its creation.

| | | |
|---:|:---:|:---|
| STARS | ✪ | **4/8** |
| STORY | 📖 | **3/8** |
| CREATIVITY | 💡 | **6/8** |
| ACTING | 🎭 | **7/8** |
| QUALITY | 🏅 | **6/8** |

The film suggests that Mary Shelly, who wrote the original Frankenstein novel, was merely relating events that occurred around 1817. This is what our lead, a time traveler from 2031, discovers shortly before he comes in contact with Victor Frankenstein and his creation. What follows is a crime procedural and too much second-hand compositing...

You have to give Frankenstein Unbound credit for taking its own direction, sticking to its aesthetic choices and not delivering the same tale for the nth time. That said, the film has such a complex story in store that it neglects its own attempts at suspense and horror in the process. As a result, the directing comes out distant, emotionless, putting talented actors in an untoward position.

The main problem, here, is that we have two movies in one. The recipe tastes bad and the ambiance is close to inexistent. The last act is the strongest one but the film never truly redeems itself. The monster doesn't get enough screen time, isn't threatening and could have used a better design. The weird telefilm photography isn't helping matters. You'll forget this film in a week...

## #29
# FRANKENSTEIN

## 1994

A monster created from human remains seeks revenge when his maker rejects him.

STARS **4/8**
STORY **3/8**
CREATIVITY **7/8**
ACTING **7/8**
QUALITY **6/8**

This unusual and sometimes frustrating rendition of Frankenstein has a made-for-television look and feel likely to rub some the wrong way. We meet Doctor Frankenstein as he invents his infamous resuscitation device. We get to meet his wife, too, who plays a significant role in previous adaptations. In a nutshell, this is the dramatized version of a story once assigned to horror realm.

This is one of many revisions to the 1818 dark publication. It's a period piece painted with a surreal vibe. It's dynamic enough that we don't get lost in dialog, but, as an epic, it lacks energy and an additional polish. The classic monster is played by Robert De Niro who's given nothing to impress us with. His make-up is striking but not scary or memorable. His character is downright boring.

1994's Frankenstein does something unique with a story retold one time too many, but has a melodramatic script and a beige ambiance that prevent it from being better. It is a poor period piece with no true historical value despite its premise, but it is meant to feel authentic and realistic. It is perfect for the Frankenstein completist, but everyone else will blame this mess on the 90's...

## #30

# VAN HELSING

## 2004

A beast hunter is caught in a war between good and evil.

STARS  6/8

STORY 6/8

CREATIVITY 8/8

ACTING 8/8

QUALITY 8/8

This outstanding production by an expert in the paranormal adventure mixed subgenre, Stephen Sommers, unites all the classic monsters and gives them a steampunk edge. Dracula, his brides, Frankenstein, his monster, Igor, Mr. Hyde, werewolves, to name a few, are at war, here; a war between good and evil that Van Helsing, beast hunter, is stuck in the middle of.

If you accept 3-D characters, a glossy polish, and if this kind of epic rubs you the right way, then it will be the perfect film and you will be mesmerized. Otherwise, like most of us, you might still enjoy it but find it too lengthy. Van Helsing is a perpetual roller coaster ride punctuated with short dialogue, romance, humor and whatever helps us catch our breath.

This script is ambitious. The actors give superior performances and deserve a medal for coping with so many effects. We're, at all times, submerged in a romanticized dimension. Not much, here, happens in the real world. In fact, this is a world of color keying and fake sets. Van Helsing comes fully equipped with weapons and gadgets that couldn't possibly exist when this film takes places.

## #31
# FRANKENSTEIN: DAY OF THE BEAST

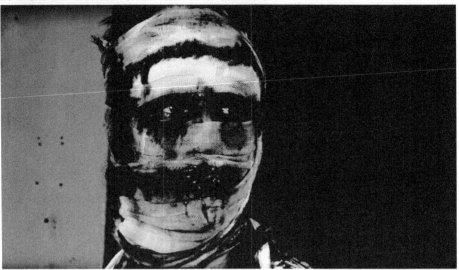

## 2011

A supernatural creature threatens a scientist, his guards and his bride.

STARS ★ **3/8**
STORY 📖 **3/8**
CREATIVITY 💡 **6/8**
ACTING 😀 **4/8**
QUALITY 🎖 **4/8**

The period piece treatment never really sinks in. The accents are fake and increasingly annoying. It doesn't help that the dialogue feels like it has been written by a teenager and it's a shame the audio and the photography are so badly rendered because underneath it all hides one of the most interesting adaptations of the famous Mary Shelley horror novel... at least on paper.

The monster is interesting; he's neither a simple brute nor a zombie. You can tell that the makers really tried to give it an interesting arc. There are hundreds of Frankenstein flicks out there, but what separates Day of the Beast from all of them is its gore. Judging by the grain and the poor lighting, you think you're watching a conservative TV movie but this couldn't be further from the truth.

You could call this a Friday the 13th of the Renaissance except for a few factors: 1) The protagonists turn against each other. 2) They use guns 3) Most are mercenaries. 4) They don't have premarital sex. 5) They don't do drugs. Joking aside, Jason Voorhees was probably a strong inspiration when it came to fleshing out this version of Frankenstein's monster, but it's still a creature of its own.

**#32**

# FRANKENWEENIE

## 2012

A boy attempts to bring back his dog to life using electricity.

STARS  **6/8**

STORY **6/8**

CREATIVITY **8/8**

ACTING **8/8**

QUALITY **8/8**

Frankenweenie is a 3D stop-motion animated feature film, which means that the stop-motion effects were simulated by a 3D software and during compositing phases to come up with a unique style. The music is by Danny Elfman and Tim Burton is directing. This is in fact the remake of one of his short stories by the same name. The original Frankenweenie was released in 1984.

The animation is not only competent but it is unlike everything we've seen. The story takes place in a parallel world where every night there's a storm, which is convenient because we're going to need lots and lots of lighting to bring back the dead! As the title implies, this is a re-imagining of Frankenstein by Mary Shelley. Victor and Igor are here, and let's not forget the monster(s).

The characters all look sick and spooky, even the kids. This is a fun film that goes in dark places. It is a horror movie for children, which doesn't mean that adults will feel excluded. It's a gateway to dark cinema. There are nods to scary films everywhere. Martin Short and Winona Ryder play significant roles. The acting is excellent. Watch out for that third act. It's uncanny!

# #33
# ARMY OF FRANKENSTEINS

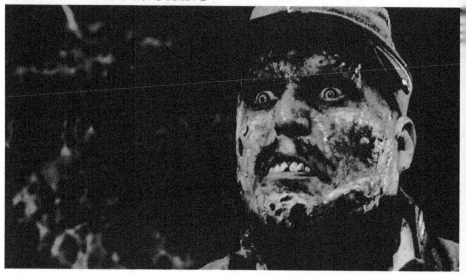

## 2013

Two men are sent back in time to the American Civil War where an army of monsters has emerged from a portal.

STARS ✪ **3/8**

STORY 📖 **3/8**

CREATIVITY 💡 **8/8**

ACTING 🎭 **5/8**

QUALITY 🏅 **4/8**

We're not talking, here, about an army of mad scientists but a revenant horde, rather. The erroneous title can lead to confusion and so can the convoluted plot. In this steampunk adaptation of Mary Shelley's Frankenstein, time travelers revisit Civil War to fix a few things. Their quest is ludicrous but fun to watch. This is a low quality movie that tries very hard to stand out, and it does.

The special effects are cheap but aren't your typical b-movie tricks. Director Ryan Bellgardt thinks outside the box, giving the feature an interesting role playing game vibe. Most of the cast is young; sometimes too young for their part. Fake mustaches, bad color keying, cheap set design, weak dialog; this is a flawed production that is much more annoying than it is charming, sadly.

This is a gorefest with slapstick violence and blood that is too red. The makers didn't take themselves or their film too seriously so we shouldn't either. It contains two cute love stories, sympathetic characters and a certain cool factor. Sure, the creature make-up looks terrible and the humour is childish, but this is as creative as Frankenstein flicks get.

## #34

# I, FRANKENSTEIN

## 2014

A revenant is stuck in a war between gargoyles and demons.

STARS ⛤ **5/8**

STORY 📖 **6/8**

CREATIVITY 💡 **8/8**

ACTING 🎭 **8/8**

QUALITY 🏅 **8/8**

This is an adaptation of Mary Shelley's Frankenstein by name mostly. We follow undead creature Adam; Frankenstein's monster, from the medieval age to recent times, but all other aspects are made up and turned into some kind of role playing fantasy game. In this rendition of the classic novel, Frankenstein's monster fights alongside an army of gargoyles a demon horde meddling with dark science.

The first sets and wardrobes are a gorgeous mix of Gothic and medieval, a style that transpires through the rest of the film. We soon carry on to present time where keen photography is only handicapped by momentarily photo-unrealistic animations, compositing and various 3D tricks. This said, CG effects allow multiple demon vs. gargoyle war sequences that wouldn't be so breath-taking otherwise.

Swapping Gothic steampunk horror for futuristic action was a bold move but the end result is unique and entertaining. A lot of effort went into making I, Frankenstein feel like the comic book it is based on and it pays off aesthetically more than it does narratively. The script is rigid and predictable. Like Underworld and Blade, this is a cool but cold superhero/action/horror hybrid.

# #35
# VICTOR FRANKENSTEIN

## 2015

A scientist recruits an assistant to help him resuscitate a dead creature.

STARS  6/8

STORY 6/8

CREATIVITY 6/8

ACTING 7/8

QUALITY 8/8

Doctor Frankenstein needs no introduction today, but his world was never depicted this way before. This is a dark steampunk science-fiction drama sprinkled with comedy and horror; a smart concoction and a fascinating formula. What's more, while it mostly follows its own unique path, the movie contains many humorous nods to previous adaptations of the classic Mary Shelley novel.

We're get one of the most hideous renditions of Frankenstein's monster ever put on film: part-hyena, part-monkey and part-dog. This said, this is Frankenstein and Igor's story and, contrary to most adaptations of this tale, there is no room for a sad monster. We get to experience the emotional, scientific, legal and political aspects of the human characters but the monster comes second.

Sympathetic and energetic, Radcliffe and McAvoy are an impressive duo that keeps us fascinated from beginning to end. The wardrobes, props and set design are sublime and contribute to an immersing experience that has us hooked. There are few slow moments but the pacing is generally tight and the ambiance is mostly tense. This is a stressful delight you won't want to miss!

## #36

# FRANKENSTEIN VS. THE MUMMY

## 2015

A mummy and a revenant terrorize a medical university.

STARS 🟊 **5/8**

STORY 📖 **5/8**

CREATIVITY 💡 **8/8**

ACTING 🎭 **6/8**

QUALITY 🏅 **6/8**

Frankenstein, here, is too preppy and too cool to fill the shoes of a teacher, an intellectual or a scientist, yet he represents all these archetypes. He finds himself a girlfriend and gets emotional quickly in order to serve the script, which makes the dialogue phony. We need to get all this exposition out of the way because we're setting the table for a duel between two monsters... at some point.

Meanwhile, the acting isn't exactly stellar but the cast is at least sympathetic. Colorful characters guide us through a story that takes a while to pick up but thankfully satisfies with its realistic gore and creature effects. This is not a Gothic period piece; it is a refreshing interpretation that takes place in the present time and makes the best of modern architecture and technology.

The film has an unusual pacing and could be shorter. It could use tighter editing. The story simply just isn't that complicated and ends up dragging or turning in circles. Also, constant use of close ups restricts the viewer's mind. This may solve financial constraints regarding set design, but it leaves the brain begging for more. Expect a cheap but decent little cross-over made skillfully.

## #37

# FRANKENSTEIN

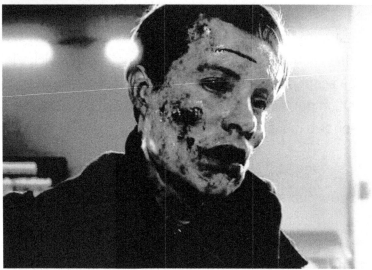

## 2015

A couple of scientists create a monster.

| | | |
|---:|:---:|:---|
| STARS | ✪ | **6/8** |
| STORY | 📖 | **6/8** |
| CREATIVITY | 💡 | **6/8** |
| ACTING | 😀 | **7/8** |
| QUALITY | 🏅 | **7/8** |

This is a modern adaptation of Mary Shelley's novel. Adam is the name of Frankenstein's revenant, for lack of a better word. He drinks milk from a bottle and is shown how to feed, shortly before he can stand, walk, then bleed and punch his way through this movie. Nothing scientific is ever explained to us and we experiment this story alongside a monster that is, apparently, both good and evil.

The film is extremely gory. This tragic tale closely transposes the events of 1931's Frankenstein in our times. The monster is given life in a laboratory. He eventually throws a little girl into a lake. He's almost killed by a bunch of corrupted cops, then by a crowd. Having things happen in 2015 makes the story more relatable than some adaptations have been.

Bernard Rose does it again. He writes and directs this film with admirable skills. Xavier Samuel creates his own type of revenant; a being that is poorly articulated but who possesses the strength of ten men. He is both vulnerable and dangerous for the same reasons. His version of the monster narrates his story from what seems like a close future, which comes with multiple commentaries on society.

*#38*

# SHARKENSTEIN

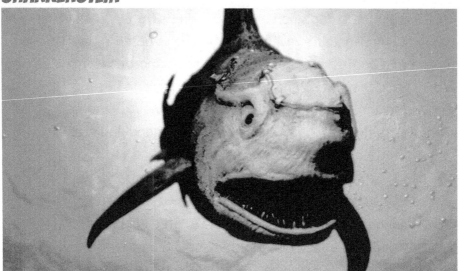

## 2016

A small ocean town is plagued by a bloodthirsty animal, reanimated using parts of sea creatures.

STARS **2/8**

STORY **2/8**

CREATIVITY **6/8**

ACTING **2/8**

QUALITY **2/8**

Sharkenstein is a film with such a big scope that it would need a significantly bigger budget to accomplish half of what it sets out to do. It's one of the worst shark week contestants there are, and that's saying a lot. This one would be perfect for a drinking game. There's no way to take any of it seriously, which could've fooled me in the first scenes. Comedy was the way to go.

The accents are ridiculous. The main casting is badly assorted and is comprised of people who couldn't possibly be friends. The shark looks like a paper cut-out, when it doesn't look like shit. The underwater shots look great, but they're probably stock footage, because they're the only thing that works. This is lazy filmmaking, to say the least. It's a waste of effort.

James Carolus plays Skip, a man half his age who wears his cap sideways... because he's a teenager. Titus Himmelberger is Coop, a man without a personality. Greta Volkova; Madge, is easy on the eyes, but lets her tattoos, braids and black cat pantyhose do the acting. She's the best thing about this movie. The truth is, these characters are atrociously written.

# #39
# DEPRAVED

## 2019

A field surgeon suffering from PTSD makes a man out of body parts and brings him to life.

STARS 6/8
STORY 6/8
CREATIVITY 6/8
ACTING 7/8
QUALITY 6/8

In Depraved, Larry Fessenden gives us his very own Frankenstein. The scientist, Henry, is played by David Call, and his creature, the guy he stitched together with body parts, is played by Alex Breaux. We never really spend time admiring how effortlessly Henry built Adam. We kind of skim over the details of his miracle. That's just not where Fessenden wants our attention spent.

This story has been told many times before, but never quite like this. Some would call this adaptation Cronenbergian, some would call it psychotronic, or body horror; some would praise it for its modernity. At the turn of the decade, this film feels very much of its time. It's in the score, the soundtrack, the use of fractal imagery, the editing that never lingers.

This only turns into a horror movie two thirds into the script, as Adam kills someone. The character we invested ourselves in, as it turns out, is led by instincts only. Duh. Revenants aren't exactly reliable. The third act is a bit of a disappointment. It's anticlimactic. Sadly, when this horror movie blooms, it also loses its mojo. Anyways, great acting, great script, a must-see!

FOR MORE HORROR-THEMED BOOKS, VISIT
WWW.TERROR.CA

Made in the USA
Coppell, TX
07 October 2021